WITHDRAWN

TRANSPORTATION
Inventions
MOVING OUR WORLD FORWARD

Robert Walker

Crabtree Publishing Company

www.crabtreebooks.com

Author: Robert Walker
Publishing plan research and development:
Reagan Miller
Editors: Renata Brunner Jass, Rachel Eagen
Copy editor: Dimitra Chronopoulos
Proofreader: Janice Dyer
Editorial services: Clarity Content Services
Design: Pixel Hive Studio
Cover design: Ken Wright
Photo research: Linda Tanaka
Project coordinator and prepress technician:
Samara Parent
Print coordinator: Margaret Amy Salter
Series consultants:
Professor D. Eric Walters, Ph.D.
Rosalind Franklin University of Medicine and Science
Jane Hutchison, Masters of Education

Front cover: Wright brothers' flyer (top right); the Buran spacecraft in Samara, Russia (bottom left); high-speed commuter train (bottom right)
Back cover: 1910 style antique car

Photographs: front cover top right Brad Whitsitt/shuttestock, bottom right cybrain/shutterstock, bottom left FotografFFF/shutterstock; back cover James Steidl/shutterstock; p4 LC-USZ62-97842/ Library of Congress; p5 bumihills/shutterstock; p7 NASA; p8 Jane Rix/shutterstock; p9 Tom Fakler/shutterstock; p10 *The Fairman Rogers Four-In-Hand (A May Morning in the Park)* by Thomas Eakins, Saint Louis Art Museum; p12 Georgios Kollidas/shutterstock; p14 LC-USZ62-29461/Library of Congress Prints and Photographs Division Washington, D.C. 20540 USA; p15 LC-USZ62-96202/ Copyright by Charles Bauer/Library of Congress; p17 LC-USZ62-110411/Library of Congress Washington, D.C. 20540 USA; p18 LC-USZ62-48300/Library of Congress Prints and Photographs Division Washington, D.C. 20540 USA; p19 Department of Transportation. Highways historical collection. RG 14-162-2-27 Archives of Ontario; p20 Roy & Danielle/CCL; p21 Used by permission of Bjørn Christian Tørrissen; p23 GFDL CC-BY-SA Geni/CCL LC-USZ62-110384/Library of Congress Washington, D.C. 20540 USA; p24 Jorg Hackemann/ shutterstock; p25, 26 Photos.com/ Thinkstock; p27 LC-DIG-ggbain-04178/Library of Congress Prints and Photographs Division Washington, D.C. 20540 USA; p30 Hemera/ Thinkstock; p31 LC-B2-5765-9/Library of Congress Prints and Photographs Division Washington, D.C. 20540; p32 NASA/Carla Thomas; p33 NASA; p1, 34 iStockphoto/Thinkstock; p35 Patrick Poendl/shutterstock; p36 Photo courtesy of Ultra Global Ltd.; p37 CCL/Khalidshou at en.wikipedia; p38 left OAR/National Undersea Research Program/Woods Hole Oceanographic Institute, Gulf of Alaska 2004/NOAA Office of Ocean Exploration; p39 iStockphoto/ Thinkstock; p40 NASA; p41 Photo by Mark Greenberg/Virgin Galactic; p42 top Everett Collection/ shutterstock, NASA Langley Research Center.

Library and Archives Canada Cataloguing in Publication

Walker, Robert, 1980-, author
Transportation inventions : moving our world forward /
Robert Walker.

(Inventions that shaped the modern world)
Includes index.
Issued in print and electronic formats.
ISBN 978-0-7787-0223-8 (bound).--ISBN 978-0-7787-0240-5 (pbk.).--
ISBN 978-1-4271-9426-8 (pdf).--ISBN 978-1-4271-9422-0 (html)

1. Transportation--Juvenile literature. 2. Technological innovations--
Juvenile literature. I. Title.

HE152.W25 2013   j388   C2013-906252-1
C2013-906253-X

Library of Congress Cataloging-in-Publication Data

CIP available at Library of Congress

Crabtree Publishing Company

www.crabtreebooks.com   1-800-387-7650

Printed in Canada/102013/BF20130920

Published in Canada
Crabtree Publishing
616 Welland Ave.
St. Catharines, ON
L2M 5V6

Published in the United States
Crabtree Publishing
PMB 59051
350 Fifth Avenue, 59th Floor
New York, New York 10118

Published in the United Kingdom
Crabtree Publishing
Maritime House
Basin Road North, Hove
BN41 1WR

Published in Australia
Crabtree Publishing
3 Charles Street
Coburg North
VIC, 3058

Contents

What Is Transportation?

On the Move

From the earliest times, humanity has been on the move. Once we only walked or rode animals. Now we ride bicycles, drive cars, fly airplanes, and travel into outer space. The evolution of transportation has changed and shaped the way we live, work, and play.

People in the United States spend almost 100 hours traveling to and from work each year. More than 90 percent of Americans rely on their feet, bicycles, cars, buses, and trains during their daily **commute**. But getting to and from work or school isn't the only reason for traveling. We travel to visit friends and family. We also travel for vacation and recreation. Early humans didn't have modern forms of transportation. How did people get around before these inventions?

People and animals provided the power for the earliest modes of transportation.

Animal Power

Early humans were **nomadic** by nature. The need for food, shelter, and avoiding harsh weather in certain seasons made them move from place to place. Hunters and gatherers walked or ran great distances in search of food.

Dogs were the first animals to be **domesticated** by people. They were used for hunting and for pulling sleds. The next big step in transportation came with the use of larger animals for travel. We have evidence that people used horses to travel and transport goods in central Asia around 3500 BCE. Animals commonly used at this time were horses, cattle, yaks, and camels. This development allowed for people to travel farther, faster.

↑ *People still use animals for transportation and work.*

Moving On

Transportation is the movement of people and things from one place to another. We may travel short distances or great ones. And we still travel by foot and animal. But through the ages, human imagination has brought new and exciting means of transport.

We built wooden boats to cross great distances over the world's oceans. The wheel allowed us to cross the land. We have created ways to fly aircraft into the sky and beyond. Whatever our reason for traveling, none of our modern modes of transport would be possible without human imagination and innovation.

What Drives Us?

What is the main driving force behind the ideas and developments in the world of transportation? Sometimes we seek the solution to a problem. Want to move something heavy? Use a sturdy wheeled vehicle. Want to cross a body of water? Travel safely and quickly in a boat. In other instances, transportation is designed to make modern life easier. Airplanes crisscrossing our skies are a perfect example of the comfort and convenience that transportation **technology** provides. Now, we can cross the greatest distances around the world in a relatively short time.

Changes in transportation are the result of discovery, invention, and innovation.
- Discovery happens when people find or learn something for the first time.
- Invention happens when people design and build something new.
- Innovation happens when someone studies an invention and then makes changes to it. An innovator uses an existing design to create something new.

None of our modern modes of transportation would be possible without the imagination and inspiration of talented inventors. Through their own discoveries, or starting with the work and ideas of others, creative men and women continue to refine the world of transportation.

Not every invention and innovation has come from the most likely of places. Not every inventor had wealth or an advanced education. They simply possessed the curiosity and determination needed to create and learn from the world around them. Take Orville (1871–1948) and Wilbur Wright (1867–1912), who never finished high school. Together, these two men were the first to successfully launch an aircraft into flight.

Where Things Can Take Us

Transportation has helped us discover the amazing world around us. It has also shaped the way we live today. We continue to move around a lot, but now we have many **vehicles** to help us do so.

In many places, food and other necessities are just a quick drive to the grocery store. We use bikes to get to school, or large trucks to move to a new city. Even exploring space is becoming possible for people who aren't astronauts. The modern age of transportation offers people a limitless potential for growth, discovery, and knowledge.

↓ Innovations in transportation arise from group efforts. For example, many people worked to design, build, test, and operate the engine shown below. It was used to power NASA's first exploration vehicles to the moon.

CHAPTER ONE

On the Road

The earliest modes of land transportation owe everything to the wheel. It may not seem that important, but without the wheel you couldn't even move dirt in a wheelbarrow. Before the wheel, all transportation happened on foot or on the backs of large animals.

The Wheel

One of the earliest recorded birthplaces of the wheel was ancient Mesopotamia, in what is now Iraq. Before the wheel, people pulled wooden sleds to move things or used rafts to float heavy items along rivers. The first wheels were made of solid wood. These were very heavy and hard to move. There were also few well-maintained roads to travel on. Most Mesopotamians preferred using rivers and sleds.

Using **spokes** helped to make wheels lighter, because a spoked wheel contains less material than a solid wheel. The development of the spoked wheel happened at the same time as the creation of the chariot around 3000 BCE. The chariot was a two-wheeled cart pulled by a horse. It was a convenient, lightweight, and fast way to move people and things. This vehicle also had a huge impact on the military as a new and effective tool in battle.

↓ *The use of spokes helped to keep wheels round, in addition to making them lighter.*

↑ *The early Roman roads were made of carefully laid stones. While easier than riding on dirt, they probably still made for a loud and bumpy ride.*

The First Roads

People walking, riding horseback, or using wheeled vehicles travel more easily on a stone surface. Around 312 BCE, the people of ancient Rome started building 50,000 miles (80,467 km) of stone roads. The first of these Roman roads was the Appian Way. It ran southeast from Rome, in a straight line, for 35 miles (56 km) to the west coast city of Terracina. It eventually extended across southern Italy to the east coast city of Brindisi—a completed length of 348 miles (560 km).

As Rome grew, so did its road systems. These connected roadways eventually linked Rome to places in Great Britain, Greece, and North Africa. Stone roads made trade and travel between distant communities faster and easier. They also made it easier for Rome's armies to travel across the Roman Empire. Everyone was free to use these roads, but each province was responsible for the repair and upkeep of its own stretch of road.

→ *Early coaches and* **carriages** *were drawn by four horses, requiring two drivers. With the four-in-hand carriage (shown here), an innovation allowed all four sets of reins to be managed by a single driver.*

Carts and Wagons

The early wheeled cart was a very simple design. It had one or two sets of wheels, a place for the driver to sit, and a small, flat area to transport people or goods. Carts were not built for comfort, but for **utility**. Wheeled carts were developed in many places around the world.

In the 1500s, the first four-wheeled coaches made their appearance in Eastern Europe. These were more comfortable to ride in than simple carts. The **stagecoach** was particularly built for comfort and style. Passengers sat on cushioned seats in an enclosed cabin. The stagecoach became very popular, especially with the upper classes in Britain. Stagecoach businesses soon popped up across Europe.

In North America, the covered wagon played a large role in the transportation of people and goods. It was originally built in an area of Pennsylvania that shared land with the Conestoga Indians. It was a very large cart, requiring six horses to move it. People used covered wagons to settle the American West.

People of the lower and middle classes didn't have the money to buy and maintain horses and private coaches. The idea of a stagecoach for hire developed, so people could rent horses and coaches for a period of time. This was the model for modern taxicabs.

Velocipedes and Bicycles

The earliest working velocipede was invented in 1817. It was called the draisine, after its inventor, Baron Karl von Drais (1785–1851). The word *velocipede* means "fast foot." Velocipedes had two wheels and were moved by the rider pushing his or her feet along the ground.

In the 1860s, bicycles were developed by adding pedals attached to the front wheel of velocipedes. James Starley (1831–1881) and William Hillman (1848–1921) built the first two-wheeled vehicles to be called bicycles, such as the Penny Farthing. It had a gigantic front wheel to let the rider travel faster. Draisines and Penny Farthings were both extremely popular for short periods, but then were declared dangerous.

John Kemp Starley (1854–1901), nephew to James, is considered the father of the modern bicycle. His innovation was known as the "safety bicycle." It was powered by a chain and gears attached to the pedal system. This bicycle also had the first air-filled rubber tires. This safer, more comfortable bicycle started a new craze, which has never gone away.

→ *The giant front wheel of some early bicycles made getting on and off difficult.*

CHAPTER TWO

Steam and Rail

The steam engine was invented to power machines. Through innovation, it was adapted to power vehicles. Before its arrival, all transportation was powered by humans or animals. The invention of the steam engine led to the development of train engines and, eventually, railroads.

↑ *James Watt invented many different things, but he is best known for his work with steam engines. He also developed the concept of* **horsepower**. *An international unit of power, the watt, is named in his honor.*

Steam Machines

In 1655, Edward Somerset (ca. 1601–1667), Second Marquess of Worcester, England, wrote a book of inventions. His book included a design for a "Water-commanding Engine," a clear **forerunner** of the steam engine. In a steam-powered engine, burning coal in a firebox creates hot gases that flow into a water-filled **boiler**. The hot gases heat the water, turning it to steam. The steam drives the engine.

In the 1700s, Thomas Newcomen (1664–1729) and James Watt (1736–1819) built the first practical machines using steam engines. These engines were used to power industrial machinery such as water pumps in mines. Watt's work allowed them to be adapted for use in transportation.

Richard Trevithick (1771–1833) was a mechanical **engineer** from Cornwall, England. In 1804, he built the first **locomotive** used to haul wagons in mines. By 1808 he had built his last locomotive, called *Catch-me-who-can*, and had improved on James Watt's engine design. Watt's engines used regular steam, which is called low-**pressure** steam. Trevithick's steam engines used high-pressure steam. This allowed them to be smaller and lighter than equally powerful low-pressure steam engines. But Trevithick's locomotives were too heavy for the rails of the time.

In 1829, George Stephenson (1781–1848) and his son Robert (1803–1859) built the *Rocket*. George was in charge of developing a railway line between Liverpool and Manchester in England. The *Rocket* was built for the Rainhill Trials, a competition to decide which locomotive would be used on the new line. The steam-powered *Rocket* easily won the competition, beating several horse-drawn and other steam-powered locomotives. This railway line was the first intercity railway to carry passengers.

James Watt
Building on the Work of Thomas Newcomen

James Watt was a Scottish engineer. While working at the University of Glasgow, Scotland, he developed an interest in the steam engine. He saw that engines of the time wasted too much energy for the power they had. This inspired him to make a more **efficient** steam engine. Watt's engines were more powerful and cost-effective. His innovations allowed the steam engine to be used in transportation.

→ *The Stephensons' Rocket locomotive ran at a speed of 29 miles (47 km) per hour. George Stephenson remained very involved in the new era of rail transportation.*

Rail Expansion

By the 1850s, steam locomotive travel was becoming increasingly popular and widespread. Rail tracks had been built between several large British cities. People continued to work with and improve steam and rail technology.

↑ *On May 10, 1869, a ceremonial Last Spike was set at Promontory Summit, Utah. This officially completed the world's first transcontinental railroad.*

In North America, engineers began designing and building their own trains, basing their work on British designs. Between 1863 and 1869, the world's first **transcontinental** railroad was built. Known at first as the Pacific Railroad, it connected the east and west coasts of the United States. It was also responsible for the growth of major cities that were built along the railroad. Another transcontinental railroad was built between 1881 and 1885 in Canada, called the Canadian Pacific Railway.

Going Underground

During the 1800s, people left the countryside and flocked to the cities looking for work. This created a lot of **congestion** on city streets, with great crowds of people and horse-drawn vehicles. With the idea of easing this congestion, engineers set about building railroad lines underground. This would be a new kind of public transportation.

The first **subway** system opened in London in 1863. By 1880, this underground railway was moving almost 40 million passengers per year. The steam-powered engine made for a smoky, smelly ride. The invention of the electric motor in 1890 solved this problem. Electric trains were powered through a third rail or from wires hanging above.

The idea for an underground rail transportation system took a little longer to catch on in the United States. In 1868,

Alfred Ely Beach (1826–1896) dug out a short tunnel beneath New York City. His plans for a subway car included a rail car powered by air pressure. Beach's idea was based on the **pneumatic** mail system used earlier in London, England. A pneumatic system is a network of tubes that uses air to push or pull objects through it.

Beach created a passenger car for what he called the Beach Pneumatic Transit Company. His first prototype was displayed at the American Institute Fair of 1867. The rail car was driven by suction in one direction, and driven in the opposite direction with a blast of air. An attempt at running a pneumatic passenger rail system in London had failed in 1846. Beach's Pneumatic Company also failed. It would be 30 years before New York City would try again to build a subway system.

 Coal-burning locomotives were the first to pull passenger cars on the subway system beneath New York City. It wasn't until 1901 that motorized cars began to replace steam-driven locomotives. By 1903, all underground subway lines were replaced with electric cars.

↓ *New York opened the seventh underground railway in the world. Work began in 1888 on the Interborough Rapid Transit line, which became the world's largest public transit system.*

CHAPTER THREE

The Automobile

For most of human history, all land vehicles were powered by people or animals. So a carriage not powered by people or animals was a revolution. The word *automobile* means "able to move by itself." In reality, of course, an automobile requires something to move it: an engine.

Horseless Carriages

People had first tried using steam power and batteries to operate "horseless carriages." The early designs, often called steamers, were simple and resembled sleds with wheels. The Stanley Steamer was a popular design. Built by twin brothers Francis (1849–1918) and Freelan O. Stanley (1849–1940), this vehicle was very fast for its time. It set a record at the Daytona Florida course for the fastest mile, at 28.2 seconds. It could travel nearly 127 miles (204 km) per hour!

But steam-powered vehicles had drawbacks. They required regular stops to refill a boiler with water. Steamers were made with lightweight parts that couldn't withstand the rough roads of the day. And steam-powered engines in general were loud and smoky.

← In 1899, Francis and his wife, Flora, drove a steam-powered "Stanley steamer" up Mt. Washington, Vermont, likely as a publicity event. The steam-powered engine was located beneath the seat.

A New Kind of Engine

All engines require some form of **fuel** or energy. In steam engines, coal or wood is burned in a firebox. This heats water in another container, and the resulting steam drives the engine. In an internal combustion engine, a gas or liquid fuel is mixed with air and burned inside the engine itself. The resulting heat drives the engine. An internal combustion engine is smaller and quieter than a steam engine, and it gives off gases instead of smoke.

Belgian engineer Étienne Lenoir (1822–1900) introduced his internal combustion engine in 1858. It burned coal gas as fuel. It looked similar to a steam engine,

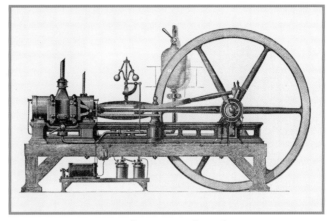

→ *Lenoir's invention of an internal combustion engine marked the dawn of the automobile and the decline of horse-drawn vehicles.*

but was smaller and more compact. Moving parts in his first engine created an electric spark, which ignited the fuel and air mixture. Lenoir's early engines were used to power pumps, mills, and printing presses. Lenoir later designed engines that ran on liquid fuels, such as gasoline.

Nikolaus August Otto (1832–1891)
Building on the Work of Étienne Lenoir

Nikolaus Otto, a German engineer, was one of many inventors to develop engines based on Lenoir's work. By 1876, Otto had constructed a more powerful version of Lenoir's engine. In it, the fuel and air mixture were compressed before being ignited. Otto's designs provided the first practical alternative to steam engines in automobiles. They also became the model for modern-day combustion engines.

The First Practical Motorcars

Karl Benz (1844–1929) is recognized by many as the inventor of the gasoline-powered automobile. In 1885 he built one of the first functioning automobiles powered by an internal combustion engine, his three-wheeled Motorwagen. His first successful attempt at the four-wheel horseless carriage was the Benz Velo, produced in 1894. This paved the way for other Benz automobiles, including a series of racing cars.

→ *In a Benz Motorwagen, one or two passengers sat between the single front wheel and the motor and two rear wheels.*

Ford and the Model T

American inventor Henry Ford (1863–1947) entered the automobile manufacturing game in 1903. The cars that were already on the road were mostly for the wealthy people who could afford them. Automobiles were made by hand and took a long time to build. Ford wanted to build a simple car that everyone could afford. To do this, he would have to manufacture more cars in the same amount of time.

Ford introduced the **assembly line** when building the Model T automobile. On an assembly line, the thing being built is moved along on a **conveyor belt**. In Ford's factory, the conveyor belt delivered a car or part to different workstations. Each worker had a simple, specific job to do or part to add. The same number of people could build more cars in the same amount of time. So, speeding up the assembly process lowered the cost per automobile.

A line taken from Henry Ford's book, *My Life and Work*:

"I spent 12 years before I had a Model T—which is what is known to-day as the Ford car—that suited me. We did not attempt to go into real production until we had a real product."

— Henry Ford, 1922

The Age of the Car

As cars became more affordable, more middle-class families bought them. Car makers worked to build simple and reliable **sedans**. Sedans had smaller engines, plenty of room for passengers, and a trunk for storing luggage.

↑ *The 1956 Federal Aid Highway Act authorized construction of the U.S. Interstate system.*

During the 1950s, the cost of a car was more than half the average family's yearly income. Yet more than 60 percent of American households owned one! People wanted to own a car and enjoy the freedom it provided. Having a car allowed people to live further from city centers and places of work. Gradually, people moved to **suburbs** away from the city cores, and eventually a car became a necessity for most families.

With so many people on the roads, more roadways were needed. Roads, bridges, highways, and tunnels were built across the country, allowing people to cross rivers, mountains, and deep canyons. Many early roads had been dirt and stone tracks, often with large potholes that made driving dangerous. A national program began to improve roads and expand networks of roads. Thus the interstate system developed, running coast to coast and border to border. There are now more than 43,000 miles (69,200 km) of U.S. highway.

 Australia's Highway 1 is the world's longest national highway system. It runs along the country's coastline, with a total length of more than 9,000 miles (15,000 km).

CHAPTER FOUR

Water: Above and Below

Most early civilizations began near lakes and rivers. This provided fresh water for drinking and for watering food crops. It was also a source of transportation for people, goods, and other items—especially before the development of stone roads.

Across the Water

Rafts made of reeds were among the earliest known watercraft. Reeds are tall, strong plants that grow in water near the shore. People probably first crossed from Southeast Asia to Australia about 50,000 years ago on rafts made of reeds and bamboo logs. The oldest known remains of reed rafts, from 5000 BCE, were found in Kuwait. The ancient Egyptians had begun using rafts for water travel by 4000 BCE. And in the Andes Mountains of South America, reeds have been used to build rafts and fishing boats for thousands of years.

↑ Traditional fishing boats in Peru are made from reeds.

People around the world also developed skin boats, which were made by stretching dried animal hides over wooden frames. Such boats were prone to breaking because of rough water or hitting rocks, but were fairly easy to repair. Other early builders carved canoes out of tree trunks. In other words, boat builders used whatever they had available to make their vessels. But such vessels were relatively small with little room for people and other things.

Larger vessels were later developed, allowing people to travel further and carry more goods. Eventually, trade grew between distant places and cultures via water travel.

Smooth Sailing

The ancient Egyptians navigated the Nile River by boat as early as 4000 BCE. Their early sailing vessels had square sails. A new kind of sail, called a **lateen**, later appeared on vessels in the Mediterranean and the Far East. Its triangular shape allowed it to be rigged, or set up, to catch the wind from more than one direction. This allowed people to sail in different weather conditions, and also out across the enormous oceans.

Further north, the Vikings became excellent sailors around 900 BCE. They sailed the seas in large, wooden **longships**. The shape of the vessel allowed it to move easily through the water. The Vikings could use either sails or oars to move their boats. These long-distance vessels made it possible for Vikings to establish settlements in Britain, France, Germany, and even across the Atlantic Ocean, in Greenland and North America.

↓ *The basic design of the Viking longship is still used in boat building today. Many ancient longships have been found and are now in museums.*

Going Under

In 1580, William Bourne (1535–1582) designed an enclosed vehicle that could be rowed underwater. The design included a wooden frame that was encased in a waterproof leather skin. But Bourne never built the ship. In 1605, another group of inventors used Bourne's plans to build the **submarine**. Unfortunately the experiment ended in failure when the vessel ran **aground** in the muddy river bottom.

Successful Submarines

Dutch inventor Cornelius van Drebbel (1572–1633) built an "underwater raft" in 1620. This became the world's first working submarine, diving as deep as 15 feet (about 4.5 m) beneath the surface. Drebbel's submarine had a wooden frame, a waterproof leather cover, and oars that came out the sides of the vessel. Bags made out of pigskins were connected by tubes to the hull. The skins were filled with water to submerge the vehicle, or allow it to move down under the water. To surface, or come back up, the water was forced out of the bags.

Drebbel later built larger submarines. But no one showed much interest in his work at the time. Later, other innovators would try to make a submarine. One based on a design by Italian Giovanni Borelli (1608–1679) was built decades later, around 1749. Similar to Drebbel's pigskins, Borelli's design used goat skins that were built into the **hull** and connected to an opening in the floor of the vessel.

Robert Fulton, of steamboat innovation fame, also tried his hand at building a submarine. His machine was called the *Nautilus* and was made of steel. It had a sail on top for traveling on the ocean surface.

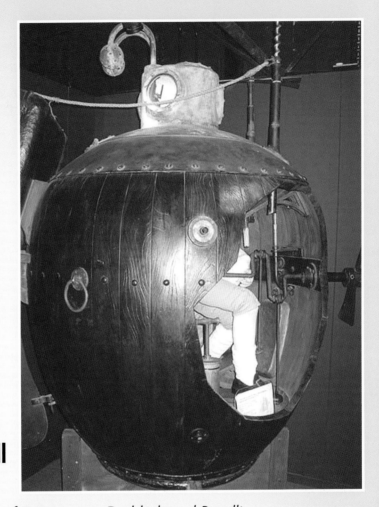

→ This life-size copy of the Turtle has a section cut away to show how the driver would sit inside. This model is displayed at the Royal Navy Submarine Museum in Gosport, England.

David Bushnell (1740–1824)

Building on the work of Bourne, van Drebbel, and Borelli

One of the biggest obstacles to the development of submarines was how to get them to move. The *Turtle* was the first American military submarine, developed by inventor David Bushnell in 1775, during the American Revolutionary War. The *Turtle* was a one-man **submersible**, powered by a **propeller**. A second vertical propeller moved the *Turtle* to the desired depth. The *Turtle* was designed to sink enemy ships to break up the British blockade of New York's harbor. However, there is no record telling us whether it was ever used successfully.

→ *Many paddlewheel steamboats are still used today, offering luxury and entertainment to their passengers.*

The Steamboat

Frenchman Claude-François-Dorothée de Jouffroy (1751–1832), the Marquis d'Abbans, was the first to use a steam-driven engine in a ship. He first used a Newcomen steam engine. In 1776, he adapted a Watt engine for a 42-foot-long (about 13 m) steamship. On some of his ships, the engine drove two **paddlewheels**.

In the United States around the same time, James Rumsey (1743–1792) and John Fitch (1743–1798) were working on steam-driven watercraft. In 1787,

Rumsey constructed a model paddleboat and tested it on the Potomac River. It reached a promising 4 **knots** (about 4.6 miles [7.4 km] per hour). Also in 1787, Fitch built America's first working steamboat. His 45-foot-long (14 m) innovation had a steam engine that powered a series of paddles. In 1788, Fitch's vessel traveled 20 miles (32 km). In a second attempt, Fitch built and launched an even larger paddleboat, which reached speeds of up to 8 knots. But Fitch did not have the funds to continue with his inventions.

Cruising in Style

In the United States, early steamships focused on luxury passenger travel. In Europe, there was great interest in creating steamers that could travel on the ocean. After all, a steam engine would allow ships to travel at any time and in any direction. The British wanted to use paddlewheel boats to carry passengers across the Atlantic Ocean.

In 1836, the Great Western Steamship Company began building the first ocean steamship, *The Great Western*. Within two years the vessel was completed. Its **maiden voyage** from England to New York City took only 15 days.

Long-distance steamers grew in size as they grew in popularity. Some of the British steamships weighed 2,000 tons or more, with three or four decks to accommodate the large number of passengers. Steam engine-powered boats slowly became the favorite mode of transportation for ocean crossings. They didn't rely on wind for **propulsion**, and could reach speeds much greater than those of sailboats.

→ *The great steamships were a revolution in world travel. For the first time in human history, large numbers of people could cross the world's oceans swiftly and in relative safety.*

Robert Fulton (1765–1815)
Building on the Work of John Fitch

The work of steamboat inventors paved the way for the paddlewheel steamboat. Like John Ford, Robert Fulton was brilliant at improving the designs of earlier inventors. In 1807, Robert Fulton's steamboat, the *Clermont*, traveled up the Hudson River from New York City to Albany. It was a huge success, and soon Fulton's boats were steaming up and down the lower Mississippi River as well.

CHAPTER FIVE

Up in the Air

The beginnings of air travel can be traced at least as far back as the 1400s. Italian artist and inventor Leonardo da Vinci designed a flying vehicle inspired by the motion of birds in flight. However, like many things he imagined, da Vinci never built this potential aircraft. But people continued to keep their eyes on the sky, working on new and interesting ways to take flight.

Balloons and Airships

When air is heated, it expands, becomes less dense, and rises. Brothers Joseph-Michel (1740–1810) and Jacques-Étienne Montgolfier (1745–1799) used this property of air when they engineered the first hot air balloon.

Air was heated by burning straw underneath the balloon opening. The Montgolfier brothers made several test flights using animals as passengers. Their first successful **crewed** flight took place in 1783.

The air inside a hot air balloon expands when heated. As the air expands, it becomes less dense than the colder air outside the balloon. When the inside air is hot enough, it causes the balloon to rise.

Scientists used early forms of flight, such as balloons, to study Earth's **atmosphere**. In 1804, French scientists Joseph Gay-Lussac (1778–1850) and Jean-Baptiste Biot (1774–1862) took a balloon to an altitude of almost 13,000 feet (3900 m). They took air samples at different altitudes to measure the differences in temperature and humidity. Rather than using hot air to get off the ground, Gay-Lussac and Biot filled the balloon with hydrogen, a lighter-than-air gas.

The next successful airship was built in 1852 by Frenchman Henri Giffard (1825–1882). Giffard constructed a gigantic, cigar-shaped vehicle. The balloon-like structure was filled with hydrogen. A large 350-pound (about 160 kg) steam engine turned a propeller for propulsion. For its maiden voyage, Giffard's creation traveled the 17 miles (27 km) from Paris to Trappes, France, at 6 miles per hour (almost 10 km/h).

Fixed Wings

Englishman George Cayley (1773–1857) built the first hand-launched glider in 1804. It was only a little more than a yard (1 m) in length and weighed very little. This marked the first time a heavier-than-air machine had fixed wings and both a horizontal and a vertical tail. Cayley later developed the first glider to fly with a passenger.

Ferdinand Graf von Zeppelin (1838–1917)

Building on the Work of Henri Giffard

The zeppelin was a large, balloon-like airship. It was named for its German aviator inventor, Ferdinand Graf von Zeppelin. Still used today, zeppelins are long, cylindrical, and filled with

↑ *Modern zeppelins are filled with helium. This gas is lighter than air and is not flammable.*

gases that are lighter than air. Zeppelins differed from other early airships because they could be steered. They were most popular from the early 1890s until the 1930s.

Experimenting with Gliders

Like many people, brothers Otto (1848–1896) and Gustav Lilienthal (1849–1933) had been interested in flight since childhood. Otto spent many years studying bird flight and building experimental aircraft. He followed George Cayley's theories regarding human flight and gliders. The Lilienthals built many different gliders using various materials and designs. Otto later published articles he wrote, and lectured about his and his brother's experiments in **aviation**.

French-born Octave Chanute (1832–1910) was an American civil engineer. He enjoyed a long career designing bridges and major railroad projects. He reportedly became interested in

aviation in 1856, when he saw a hot-air balloon take off. Chanute collected all the information he could find about aviation and had it reprinted in the book *Progress in Flying Machines* in 1894. He also worked on designing gliders between 1896 and 1898.

→ *One of George Cayley's early successful flights in a glider.*

 Some of the earliest designs for flying machines called for wings that flapped like a bird's. Unfortunately, the wingspan needed to lift a person off the ground was too large to be supported by the frames of such vehicles. These early designs usually ended in pieces on the runway.

→ *The 1913 Benoist XIV was a small "flying boat" design. Only two planes were built. They were used to provide the first heavier-than-air airline service in the world and the first U.S. airline service of any kind.*

Powered Flight

The Wright brothers are possibly the most well-known people in aviation history. Orville (1871–1948) and Wilbur (1867–1912) operated a bicycle shop in North Carolina. While they made bikes on the ground, they dreamed of flying in the air. One of their employees was mechanic Charles Taylor (1868–1956). Taylor built engines for their aircraft, including a 12-horsepower engine for their first powered flight in *Flyer 1*. Hundreds of test flights followed, with the Wright brothers constantly improving their plane designs and Taylor building engines.

The beginning of World War I furthered the development of flight powered by internal combustion engines. People on both sides of the war wanted reliable, fast airplanes that could dominate battles. By the war's end, 400-horsepower engines had replaced early 80-horsepower ones.

Wilbur and Orville Wright
Building on the Work of Cayley, the Lilienthals, and Chanute

The aviation success of the Wright brothers was based on the experiments, successes, and failures of many people. They studied George Cayley's and the Lilienthal brothers' accomplishments and publications. They corresponded frequently with Octave Chanute. Their employee, Charles Taylor, built the engine for *Flyer 1*. Together, the Wrights and Taylor completed *Flyer 1* in 1903, after four years of work.

→ *Da Vinci never actually built the aerial screw. Experts today believe that it would not have flown.*

From Aerial Screws to Helicopters

Leonardo da Vinci first devised the idea of a helicopter around 1483. His design was called the **aerial** screw. On it, a screw-shaped structure would "screw" into the air above, causing lift off. The aerial screw would have required several men to turn the cranks to make the propellers spin.

French engineer Paul Cornu (1881–1944), a bicycle maker, designed and built the first crewed helicopter. Cornu built his machine to take part in an aviation contest in 1907. It consisted of a four-wheeled cart driven by a 24-horsepower engine. The machine achieved flight for less than half a minute. Cornu abandoned the project after this early accomplishment.

American helicopter inventor Igor Sikorsky's hopes for his invention:

"I always believed that the helicopter would be an outstanding vehicle for the greatest variety of life-saving missions."

— Igor Sikorsky, 1972

Spinning Along

Huge leaps in the world of helicopter transportation were made during World War II. The first working helicopter, the Focke-Wulf 61, was built by German inventor Heinrich Focke (1890–1979) and first flown in 1936. It had two large **rotors**, one on each side of the machine. Based on the success of his first model, Focke set about designing and building the Focke-Achgelis Fa 223. It was much larger than the Focke-Wulf 61. It had a powerful 1000-horsepower BMW engine. The Focke-Achgelis Fa 223 set records for speed, altitude, and distance. Later it became the first helicopter to be flown across the English Channel.

American engineer Igor Sikorsky (1889–1972) built the VS-300 in 1939. It was the first helicopter to have a large overhead rotor and small tail rotor. The VS-300 was a success.

→ In this early version of a helicopter, the pilot increased power to the main rotor, on top to take off. To land, the pilot reduced power to the main rotor. To fly forward, the pilot used a control that tilted the main rotor forward.

The U.S. Army ordered 133 R-4s, a later model designed by Sikorsky. The R-4 helicopter was soon being used in rescues. In 1944, one was used to fly medical supplies through stormy weather to the survivors of a ship explosion. This was the first lifesaving mission involving a helicopter.

Helicopters are uniquely suited to lifesaving missions. They can land in places other aircraft cannot, such as a city street or the rooftop of a hospital. And they can hover in one spot, making them useful for rescue operations on land or at sea.

Of Jet Engines . . .

Jet engines are another type of internal combustion engine. They draw in air through the front of the engine and **compress** it. The air then mixes with fuel in the combustion chamber, where the fuel ignites. The resulting explosion of hot gases moves out of the rear of the engine, pushing the aircraft forward.

The first jet engine was designed in 1928 by British engineer Frank Whittle (1907–1996). However, it took Whittle nine years to build a working engine. It was called the Whittle Unit (WU) engine. Jet engines have mostly replaced propeller propulsion in aircraft because they allow planes to travel much faster and over greater distances.

Early **commercial** flights were very expensive, and did not allow for long continent- or ocean-crossing voyages. Jet engines revolutionized air travel. By the 1970s, cheaper, more affordable flights were available. Soon dozens of airlines competed to offer travel over greater distances and in greater comfort. Giant planes such as the Boeing 747 started crisscrossing the globe, carrying up to 416 passengers at a time.

A Boeing 747 is so large and powerful, NASA used a specialized one to transport its Space Shuttles between launch, landing, and service sites.

The Saturn V

Building on the work of Robert Goddard

The Saturn V rocket was used by **NASA** for the Apollo and Skylab programs. The Apollo program sent people to the moon for the first time. The chief architect of the Saturn V (pronounced "Saturn Five") program was a German immigrant named Wernher von Braun (1912–1977). Von Braun had a long career as a rocket scientist, engineer, and space architect. Robert Goddard's work served as the basis for the work of von Braun and all other rocket scientists since.

↑ *The Saturn V was the most powerful rocket used to send payloads, or cargo, into space.*

. . . and Rockets

Humanity's dreams of flying didn't stop at the clouds—they carried on past Earth's atmosphere. In 1926, scientist Robert H. Goddard (1882–1945) launched the first liquid-fuel **rocket**. His accomplishment marked the beginning of modern rocketry. Liquid fuel rockets use liquid **propellant** and oxygen. As in an internal combustion engine, mixing of the liquid propellant and oxygen creates an explosion, giving off water and tremendous heat. As the water vaporizes, it expands and shoots out of the bottom of the rocket at a high speed. Using Goddard's work, people were preparing for crewed flights into space about 50 years later.

CHAPTER SIX

Transportation: Today and Tomorrow

From the earliest reed rafts to the space vehicles of today, much has happened in the evolution of transportation. Humans have continually found ever more fuel-efficient ways to travel increasingly greater distances. We now have cars that are powered by light from the sun, ships that will take us to and from the moon, and vessels that reveal the dark and mysterious ocean bottom.

Hybrid Cars

Cars have changed a lot since their first appearance more than 100 years ago. They've gotten faster, more reliable, and more fuel-efficient. The latest development, the **hybrid** automobile, is a combination of old and new engineering. A hybrid car gets its power from both a gasoline-driven internal combustion engine and an electric motor.

→ From the outside, a modern hybrid automobile looks just like any other automobile.

Automobiles of the Future

Sometime in the next 30 years, experts estimate that there will be more than 1.2 billion cars on Earth. And by 2030, an estimated 60 percent of the world's population will live in urban areas. Today's typical American automobile weighs about 4000 pounds (1814 kg) and is about 16 feet (4.9 m) long. Smaller cars will be ever more desirable in crowded city streets, reducing congestion and air pollution.

In 2012, American automaker General Motors unveiled its plans for the car of the future. The EN-V 2.0 is a two-wheeled, battery-powered car and is very compact. It weighs less than 1100 pounds (500 kilograms) and is less than 6 feet long (about 2 m). Its battery can be recharged using ordinary electrical outlets. However, when the battery is fully charged, the electric vehicle has a top speed of just 25 miles (40.2 km) per hour and can only travel about 25 miles.

↑ *The continual search for ways to make standard passenger cars smaller and more environmentally friendly is reflected in their shape and design.*

While internal combustion engines don't produce smoke like steam engines did, they do create air pollution. Smaller cars using alternative fuels are now being designed. They will address the worldwide problems of crowded city streets, declining sources of fuel, and increased pollution. But these are still in the early stages of design. It may be more than a decade before more advanced hybrids are widely available.

An Early Electric Car

One of the first electric cars was the Bushbury Electric cart. It was built in 1897 by the Star Cycle factory in Wolverhampton, England. It had three wheels, with a single front wheel controlled by a set of reins. It was powered by 2 three-speed electric motors located beneath the seat.

↑ *Each ULTra pod carries four passengers and their luggage.*

People Movers

Scientists and engineers are working on solutions to reduce congestion and air pollution in crowded cities. Personal rapid transit (PRT) devices are an example of this kind of solution.

The ULTra (Urban Light Transit) system is a PRT network that is in use at London's Heathrow Airport. Passengers and their luggage are transported in lightweight pod vehicles on specially designed pathways running between the airport terminals and parking lots. Since the vehicles are electric, there are no **emissions**, which means less air pollution.

High-speed Rail

The future of travel between urban centers is also continually evolving. High-speed electric trains move millions of people around Asia, Europe, and parts of the United States. The trains are made of lightweight materials and are designed to have a very smooth, sleek shape that allows them to cut through the air easily, with very little **air resistance**.

The world's first high-speed train route opened in 1964 in Japan. It made the trip from Tokyo to Osaka—a distance of more than 300 miles (480 km)—in four hours. This trip usually took more than 6.5 hours! And trains have only been getting faster. Japan's current high-speed Shinkansen trains are electric and travel at speeds of up to 185 miles (298 km) per hour. The Tokyo-Osaka trip is now only 2 hours and 35 minutes.

The Chinese high-speed CRH380 trains are designed to travel at more than 217 miles per hour (350 km/h). At such speeds, the driver can't read any trackside signals, which have to be transmitted to the driver's control station. For safety reasons, China's high-speed trains travel at 185 miles per hour (298 km/h).

Plans are in the works for more high-speed rail systems in Europe and North America. The California High-Speed Rail Authority has begun to develop a rail network that will run from San Francisco to Los Angeles. There are also plans for a high-speed rail system in Alberta, Canada, to run between the cities of Calgary and Edmonton.

→ The CRH380A is one of the fastest trains in the world today. During an early eight-car run, a top speed of 258.9 miles (416.6 km) per hour was reached.

New Ocean Travelers

New and improved watercraft are traveling the ocean above and below the water. Hydrofoils are high-speed boats that travel on wing-like fins located beneath the hull of the boat. When traveling at slower speeds, the boat lowers into the water. When it starts to speed up, the fins push the hull out of the water. This lets the boat to move much faster, practically flying across the water.

A lot is happening below the surface of the water, too! The Shinkai 6500 is a crewed deep-sea research vessel that can reach depths of 21,325 feet (4 miles, or 6500 m), making it one of the world's deepest diving sea exploration vehicles. The Shinkai 6500 requires two pilots to operate the vehicle, with additional room for one researcher. Its main purpose is to study geology and deep-sea life on the ocean floor.

← The U.S. National Oceanic and Atmospheric Association (NOAA) uses a small fleet of both crewed and remote-controlled deep-sea submersibles to explore the ocean.

↑ Submersibles allow scientists to make discoveries about the ocean depths. Here researchers study a dead piece of deep-sea bamboo coral.

↑ *The world economy is partly dependent on massive cargo ships that cross the oceans.*

Some ocean-going vessels are now powered with **nuclear power**. It takes two nuclear reactors to power the *USS George Washington*. The *George Washington* weighs more than 100,000 tons (90,700 metric tons), with a range of almost 200,000 miles (321,859 km). The ship has almost 6000 crew members and can support more than 80 jets and helicopters on its main deck. Nuclear-powered submarines can remain under water for months at a time without having to resurface. Nuclear submarines in the U.S. Navy Seawolf class can travel to depths of more than 1970 feet (600 m).

Large luxury cruise ships have replaced the old paddlewheel steamboats and steamships. These leisure boats cater to people wanting the adventure of being at sea, but with all the comforts of a fine hotel. One of the world's largest cruise ships has room for 3560 passengers. It has a large room for a theater, a games arcade, restaurants, and a television studio.

→ *Soyuz rockets and spacecraft transport people and materials into space—and back.*

Space Travel

The Saturn V rocket was used to send spacecraft into space. It was the most powerful launch vehicle ever built. At more than 360 feet (109.7 m) tall and weighing almost 3000 tons (2721 metric tons), it ignited in three separate stages. In the first stage, it fired for 2 1/2 minutes. In the second stage, it fired for almost 6 minutes. And the final stage fired long enough to ensure the spacecraft made it into Earth's orbit. The Saturn V allowed the United States to become the first nation to have people reach the moon's surface.

The Russian Soyuz rocket was launched in the 1960s. An extensively modernized version, Soyuz-U, was first launched in 1973. It would become the most used rocket over the next 30 years, setting a new standard for durability and reliability. Currently, all space travel is conducted using Soyuz spacecraft and rockets, which are launched into space from the Baikonur Cosmodrome in Kazakhstan.

The Soyuz was used to transport the first crew to the International Space Station (ISS) in 2000. The ISS is an orbiting laboratory where experiments are conducted in the **zero gravity** of space. The ISS has been continuously occupied since 2000. It is as big as a football field and weighs 924,739 pounds (419,455 kg). The Soyuz system is still being used to transport astronauts, materials, and supplies to and from the ISS.

A new spacecraft is being planned, called the Orion Multi-Purpose Crew Vehicle (MPCV). It may be used to support the ISS, return to the moon, and even develop crewed missions to Mars. NASA plans for the Orion spacecraft to be working by the year 2016. In the meantime, NASA and several private companies are supporting the development of commercial space travel. Ordinary people may have the opportunity to experience space travel for themselves!

↓ *A U.S. company called Virgin Galactic has designed a new kind of vehicle, called a space plane. They plan to take passengers out to experience space.*

The first "space tourist" was an American named Dennis Tito. He paid $20 million dollars to spend eight days in orbit around Earth.

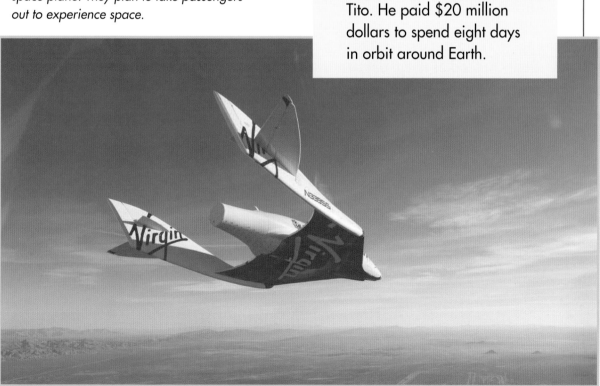

Movement is in our nature, and our history continues to shape our future. Our ancestors trekked across huge distances, relying only on the strength of their bodies. Later we learned to domesticate and train animals, such as dogs, camels, and horses to help us travel and move things. The invention of the wheel gave rise to chariots, bicycles, and automobiles. These in turn inspired the untold miles of trails, roads, and rail systems that now crisscross the planet.

The evolution of transportation has been shaped by challenges. When faced with the obstacle of oceans and rivers, we built rafts and boats to cross water. Continual innovation allowed people to travel the world as never before. Curiosity has led us to the deepest, pitch-dark depths of the ocean floor.

Eventually we found ways to travel beyond our planet. We studied a bird's wing, took flight in planes, and eventually launched into space in spacecraft. Soon humanity may travel to new worlds and frontiers.

← Humans may someday stand where we have so far only sent robots: on Mars, more than 35 million miles (56 million km) away.

Learning More

Books

Becker, Helaine. *What's the Big Idea? Inventions that Changed Life on Earth Forever.* Maple Tree Press, 2009.

Di Domenico, Kelly. *Super Women in Science* (The Women's Hall of Fame Series). Second Story Press, 2002.

Editors of YES Mag. *Robots: From Everyday to Out of This World.* Kids Can Press, 2008.

Lee, Dora. *Biomimicry: Inventions Inspired by Nature.* Kids Can Press, 2011.

Websites

America on the Move
http://www.amhistory.si.edu/onthemove/
A look at the history of transportation, focusing on the United States.

ManyThings.org: The History of Transportation in the United States
http://www.manythings.org/voa/history/249.html
The history of transportation in the United States, with informative text and photographs.

PBS: They Made America
http://www.pbs.org/wgbh/theymadeamerica/index.html
Based on a PBS television series about influential innovators in American history.

The Franklin Institute: History of Transportation Technologies
http://www.fi.edu/learn/case-files/transportation.html
A review of the most important developments in the history of transportation technologies.

Timeline

6000 BCE Scandinavian inventors design and make wooden sleds to travel on snow.

5000 BCE Early rafts and similar watercraft are commonly used.

4000 BCE The first paved streets are built in what is now Iraq.

3500 BCE The wheel is developed in Mesopotamia and several places around the world.

500 BCE Persian king Darius has the Royal Road built, a system of roads between the Persian Gulf and The Mediterranean Sea.

300 BCE Traders and travelers begin using the Silk Road, which ran 4000 miles (6437 km) between Europe and Asia.

605 China begins work on the Grand Canal system. The waterway reached a length of almost 1114 miles (1793 km), and was used to transport people and goods.

875 Abbas ibn-Firnas constructs a set of wings, attaches them to his body, and attempts to fly. He crashed, injuring his back.

1000 Viking ships are the first European ships to reach North America.

1500s The stagecoach makes its first appearance in Eastern Europe.

1673 American colonists build the Boston Post Road. It ran between Boston, Massachusetts, and New York City.

1765 Engineer James Watt invents a steam engine that will power boats and locomotives.

1775 David Bushnell builds his submarine, the *Turtle*.

1776 Claude-François-Dorothée de Jouffroy builds the first steamship.

1783 The first crewed hot air balloon takes flight.

Jean de Rozier reaches a height of over 1000 feet (305 m) in a balloon.

1785 Jean Pierre Blanchard and John Jeffries make the first balloon crossing of the English Channel.

1804 The first steam locomotive is built.

1807 The first fully functioning steamboat is launched.

1816 Baron Karl von Drais builds a bicycle with It has no pedals or gears.

1829	George and Robert Stephenson build their steam locomotive, the Rocket.
1842	George Cayley designs the Aerial Carriage, complete with rotors, propellers, and a steam engine.
1863	The first subway system opens in London, England.
	The first transcontinental railroad begins construction.
1876	The first four-stroke internal combustion engine is built by Nikolaus Otto.
1893	The first American automobile is built by Charles and Frany Duryea.
1903	The Wright brothers have success with *Flyer 1* at Kitty Hawk, North Carolina.
	Henry Ford forms the Ford Motor Company.
1906	One of the world's first trucks is built by the Brush Runabout Company of Detroit.
1907	Paul Cornu flies the first helicopter (for less than a minute).
1908	The Ford Model T goes into mass production.
1926	Robert Goddard launches the first liquid-fueled rocket.
1936	The Focke-Wulf 61, the first working helicopter, is first flown.
1956	The first interstate highway opens in Topeka, Kansas.
1960	The *Trieste* is the first crewed submersible to reach the bottom of Challenger Deep, the deepest place in Earth's oceans.
1961	The first person travels into space, Russian Yuri Gagarin.
1964	The first high-speed railroad opens in Japan.
1969	Americans Neil Armstrong and Buzz Aldrin are the first people to walk on the moon.
1971	The Amtrak rail passenger network is put into effect.
1974	The Emergency Highway Conservation Act is passed. It reduces the speed on interstate highways to 55 miles per hour (88 km/h).
1986	The first space station, the Russian *Mir*, goes into orbit.
2001	The first space tourist spends eight days on the International Space Station.
	The speedboat Vesco Turbinator reaches a speed of almost 458 miles per hour (737 km/h).

Glossary

aerial Existing, happening, or operating in the air

aground On or onto the bottom in shallow water

air resistance A force that opposes movement of objects through air

assembly line A series of workers and machines that each have a simple, specific job or task

atmosphere The layer of gases that surrounds a planet

aviation The flying or operating of an aircraft

boiler A fuel-burning container or machine for boiling water to create steam in an engine

carriages Wooden passenger vehicles pulled by horses

commercial Related to the buying and selling of goods and services

commute The regular journey to and from a place of work

compress Squeeze or press together into a smaller space

congestion An over-crowding or blocking of something, such as a road or walkway

conveyor belt A continuously moving band of fabric that carries things from one place to another in a factory

crewed Operated by people in the vehicle

domesticated Tamed and kept on a farm or as a pet

efficient Getting maximum results with the least waste or effort

emissions Substances that are given off

engineer A person who builds or maintains machines

forerunner A person or thing that exists before the development or existence of someone or something else

fuel A material burned to produce power and/or heat

horsepower A unit of power equal to 550 foot-pounds per second (a foot-pound is the energy required to raise 1 pound of material a distance of 1 foot)

hull The main body (sides and bottom) of a ship

hybrid A thing made by combining two different elements

knots Units of speed, equal to one nautical mile per hour (one nautical mile equals 2,025 yards [1,852 m])

lateen A triangular cloth sail

locomotive A powered rail vehicle used to pull a train

longships Long, shallow, wooden watercraft with sails and oars, used mainly by Vikings

maiden voyage First or earliest journey

NASA The U.S. National Aeronautical and Space Administration

nomadic Having no permanent home and moving from place to place in a pattern, usually to find food and land to feed animals

nuclear power Electric power generated by a nuclear reactor in which energy is created in controlled division of atoms

paddlewheels Steam-driven wheels that propel a ship though water

pneumatic Containing or operated by air or gas that is under pressure

pressure A force on or against an object

propellant A substance that causes something to move

propeller A mechanical device that moves a vehicle, usually two or more angled blades attached to a revolving shaft

propulsion Driving or pushing forward

rocket A cylindrical object designed to be shot through the air, to reach great heights or distance

rotors Rotating parts of a machine or vehicle; in aircraft, providing lift for takeoff

sedans Automobiles with four doors that seat four or more people and have an enclosed storage area for luggage

spokes Round bars connecting the center of a wheel to its outer edge

stagecoach A large horse-drawn vehicle with an enclosed passenger compartment

submarine An underwater, crewed vehicle

submersible A vehicle that can travel under water

suburbs The areas near but outside of a city, usually where people live

subway A railroad that runs underground

technology The application of scientific knowledge for practical purposes

transcontinental Crossing a continent, from one coast to another

utility Useful and functional, as opposed to decorative

vehicles Things used to transport people or goods, especially on land, such as carts, trucks, or cars

zero gravity The condition in which no apparent force of gravity is acting on an object

Index